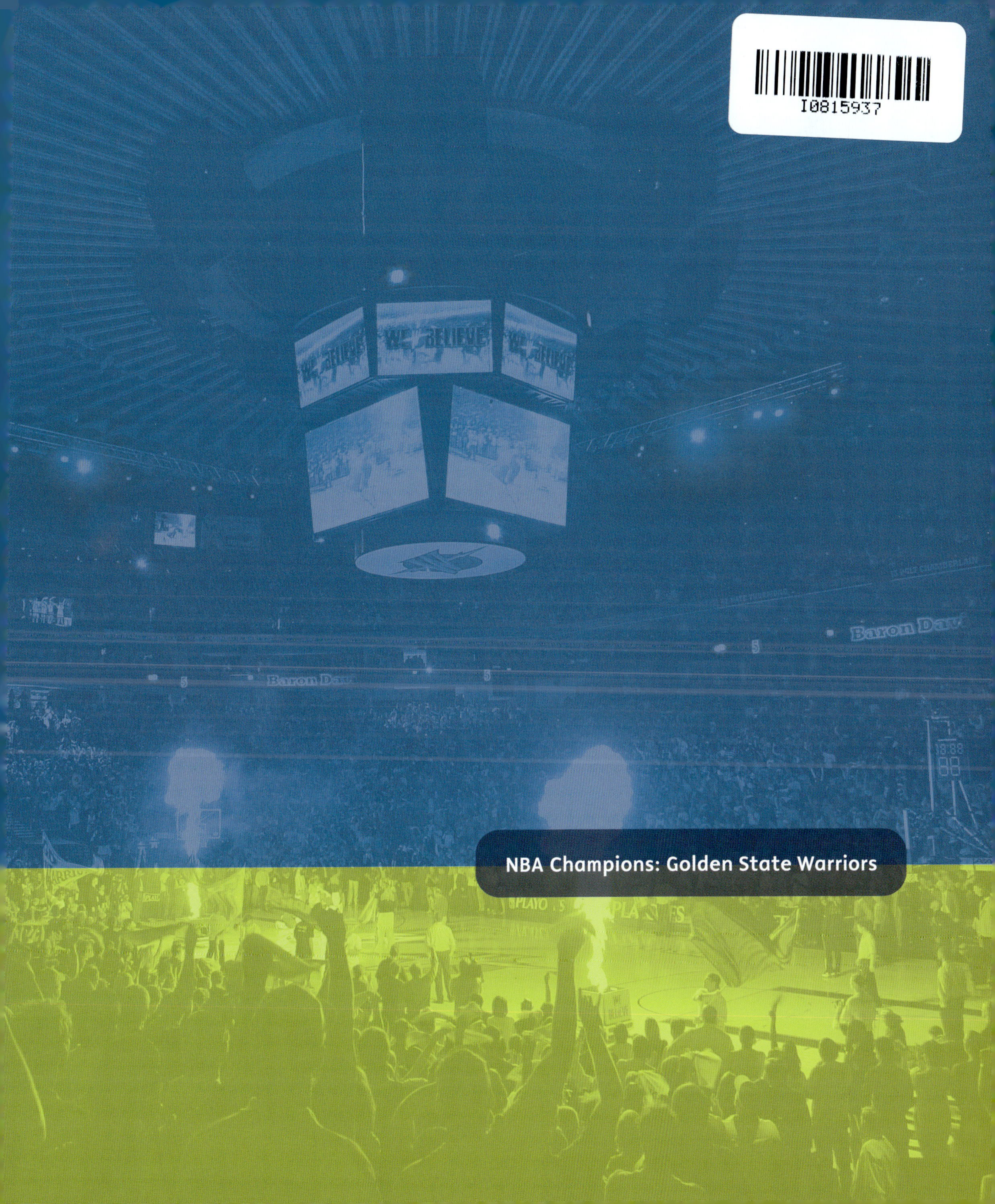
I0815937
WE BELIEVE
Baron Davis
NBA Champions: Golden State Warriors

Center Nate Thurmond

NBA CHAMPIONS

GOLDEN STATE WARRIORS

JOE TISCHLER

CREATIVE EDUCATION / CREATIVE PAPERBACKS

Center Wilt Chamberlain

Published by Creative Education and Creative Paperbacks
P.O. Box 227, Mankato, Minnesota 56002
Creative Education and Creative Paperbacks are imprints of
The Creative Company
www.thecreativecompany.us

Art Direction by Tom Morgan
Book production by Graham Morgan
Edited by Grace Cain

Images by Associated Press/Paul Vathis, 12; Getty Images/Andrew D. Bernstein, 3, 19, Bettmann, 6, Dick Raphael, cover, 5, 15, Ezra Shaw, 20, Garrett Ellwood, 1, 24, George Long, 2, Mitchell Funk, 9, Rocky Widner, 16, Thearon W. Henderson, 7, 10, Tim Heitman, cover, Walter Iooss Jr., 4

Library of Congress Cataloging-in-Publication Data

Names: Tischler, Joe, author.
Title: Golden State Warriors / by Joe Tischler.
Other titles: Creative sports: NBA champions.
Description: Mankato, Minnesota : Creative Education and Creative Paperbacks, [2025] | Series: Creative sports: NBA champions | Includes index. | Audience: Ages 7-10 | Audience: Grades 2-3 | Summary: "Elementary-level text and dynamic sports photos highlight the NBA championship wins of the Golden State Warriors, plus sensational players associated with the professional basketball team such as Stephen Curry"— Provided by publisher.
Identifiers: LCCN 2024014038 (print) | LCCN 2024014039 (ebook) | ISBN 9798889892564 (library binding) | ISBN 9781682776223 (paperback) | ISBN 9798889893677 (ebook)
Subjects: LCSH: Golden State Warriors (Basketball team)—History—Juvenile literature. | CYAC: Golden State Warriors (Basketball team)—History.
Classification: LCC GV885.52.G64 T57 2025 (print) | LCC GV885.52.G64 (ebook) | DDC 796.323/640979461—dc23/eng/20240402
LC record available at https://lccn.loc.gov/2024014038
LC ebook record available at https://lccn.loc.gov/2024014039

Printed in China

Forward Chris Mullin

Center Wilt Chamberlain

CONTENTS

Home of the Warriors

San Francisco, California, sits along the Pacific Ocean. The Golden Gate Bridge is there. So is an **arena** called the Chase Center. It's home to a basketball team called the Warriors.

The Golden State Warriors are a National Basketball Association (NBA) team. They play in the Pacific Division. That's part of the Western Conference. Their **rivals** are the Los Angeles Lakers and Sacramento Kings. All NBA teams want to win the NBA Finals and become champions. The Warriors have done so seven times!

Point guard Stephen Curry

Naming the Warriors

The Warriors began play in Philadelphia, Pennsylvania. In the 1920s, there had been a basketball team known as the Philadelphia Warriors. Owners of the new team named the team after that squad. The team kept the nickname when they moved to San Francisco in 1962.

Forward Paul Arizin

Warriors History

The Philadelphia Warriors began play in 1946. They were one of the 11 original teams of the NBA. They won the very first league championship! The team's first star was forward Joe Fulks. He led the league in scoring in 1947. Center Neil Johnston was also a great scorer. He led the Warriors to another **title** in 1956.

Center Wilt Chamberlain was one of the game's greatest players. He was the NBA **Most Valuable Player (MVP)** and Rookie of the Year in 1960.

He once scored 100 points in a game! He is the only player to average more than 50 points per game in a season.

The team moved to San Francisco in 1962. Their name was the San Francisco Warriors. The team changed its name in 1971. They were now called the Golden State Warriors. California's state nickname is the "Golden State." They won their first NBA title in California in 1975. Forward Rick Barry was a great shooter. He led the NBA in free throw percentage six times.

Forward Rick Barry

Point guard Stephen Curry

Another all-time great shooter came in 2009. His name is Stephen Curry. He is the only player in history to make over 3,000 three-pointers. Twice he has been named NBA MVP. He's led the Warriors to four NBA titles (2015, 2017, 2018, 2022).

Other Warriors Stars

The Warriors have had many great stars. Forward Paul Arizin was a great scorer. He twice led the league in scoring. He was teammates with Johnston on the 1956 title team.

Tim Hardaway, Mitch Richmond, and Chris Mullin formed a strong group in 1989. They were called "Run TMC." It was a play on the hip-hop group Run DMC. They added a lot of fun to the game.

Shooting guard Mitch Richmond

Shooting guard Klay Thompson

Guard Klay Thompson formed a backcourt bond with Curry. Together they have been called the "Splash Brothers." They both make a lot of three-point shots. Teammate Draymond Green added some muscle close to the basket. He is a great defender. Warriors fans hope these players can help the team win another championship soon!

About the Warriors

First season: 1946–47

Conference/division: Western Conference, Pacific Division

Team colors: blue and yellow

Home arena: Chase Center

NBA CHAMPIONSHIPS:

1947, 4 games to 1 over Chicago Stags

1956, 4 games to 1 over Fort Wayne Pistons

1975, 4 games to 0 over Washington Bullets

2015, 4 games to 2 over Cleveland Cavaliers

2017, 4 games to 1 over Cleveland Cavaliers

2018, 4 games to 0 over Cleveland Cavaliers

2022, 4 games to 2 over Boston Celtics

TEAM WEBSITE:

https://www.nba.com/warriors

Glossary

arena—a large building with seats for spectators, where sports games and entertainment events are held

Most Valuable Player (MVP)—an honor given to the season's best player

rival—a team that plays extra hard against another team

title—another word for championship

Shooting guard Monta Ellis

Index